Win More Sales

OVERCOMING OBJECTIONS

How to Close More Sales at Higher Margins Using Proven Strategies

by Carl Henry

Cover & Book design by Nichole Ward, Morrison Alley Design

Although the author and publisher have made every effort to ensure the accuracy and completeness of information contained in this book, we assume no responsibility for errors, inaccuracies, omissions, or any inconsistency herein. Any slights of people, places, or organizations are unintentional.

First Printing 2016

ISBN 978-0-9969360-0-2

Win More Sales Overcoming Objections

Contents

INTRODUCTION

The heat was turned up in the airport terminal, but that's not why I was starting to sweat. Outside, I could hear the wind whipping over metal, glass, and concrete, even through a thick layer of safety glass. Could a small airliner – barely more than a puddle-jumper – *really* fly in these conditions, or would we get tossed around like a kite?

I wasn't the only one second-guessing the wisdom of flying, either. In the seat next to me, I could see a clearly nervous businessman was trying to stay nonchalant while thumbing through last-minute hotel reservation options on his phone.

Finally, I walked up to the ticket counter, where a group of flight attendants was waiting to get on the plane. I got the attention of the one who seemed to be in charge, and asked her if she actually thought the flight would depart on time.

The look she gave me was one that mothers usually reserve for children who are hiding from imaginary monsters in the closet. "Don't worry," she said soothingly, "I've worked with this pilot lots of times before. We are lucky to have him today. He knows what he's doing."

The dilemma still sat in the back of my mind for a moment. I was anxious to get home and see my family, and driving would take at least three times as long. In the end, I thought about the way the flight attendant seemed completely unconcerned, and 15 minutes later I went ahead and boarded the plane.

Before takeoff, the captain had indeed come on the intercom to warn us that things might be a little bit bumpy, but that we'd soon get over the storm and everything would be fine. And sure enough, that's exactly what happened.

After a smooth landing a couple of hours later, I waited until the other twenty or so passengers had disembarked so I could have a quick word with the captain. Walking toward the cockpit, I could see he had the look of a veteran aviator, someone who had seen it all. In a different setting, he could have been a sea captain. I asked him, "That storm seemed pretty rough and we took off. Weren't you nervous?"

His reply? "If we waited for perfect weather none of our passengers would ever get anywhere. The trick is knowing the difference between a few bumps and something that's actually dangerous."

With that, we wished each other a good day and went about our business. But that idea has stuck with me ever since… and it's a great way to think about sales objections.

In a perfect world, we would identify qualified prospects, present valuable and personalized solutions to them, and then have them sign on the dotted line. We would make a fortune in sales by helping businesses and individuals get exactly what they need, at a fair price and with quality service to back it up.

Unfortunately, things don't usually work out that way. Even though we can strive to find the perfect solutions for everyone, we still have to overcome things like skepticism and competitiveness, not to mention uncontrollable factors like budgets and timelines. As a result, we have to deal with sales objections almost every day. Before we can get to the smooth landing, we have to deal with a few bumps.

And if we waited for all of those bumps to disappear, we wouldn't ever get anywhere.

Dealing with objections is part of selling, but it's something that a lot of salespeople don't know how to do very well. This is partly because they rush through the sales process and invite objections that wouldn't have come up otherwise. It also happens because they fail to understand the real nature of objections, and tend to give up on a sale too soon.

In this short book, I'm going to show you how to avoid those kinds of mistakes. Drawing on 30+ years of experience as a salesperson, coach, and trainer, I'm going to help you understand what objections are, why they come up, and what you should do about them. I'm even going to shed some light on the differences between hard objections and soft ones. In the process, we're going to see why some objections can kill a sale, but most simply mean that you have to fly over, above, or around.

By learning to understand sales objections, and to deal with them without becoming flustered, you make it possible to double, triple, or even quadruple your income in a short amount of time. So why wait any longer? Let's start seeing sales objections for what they really are...

" *You can't become*
a top salesperson
if you don't master objections…
and you can't master objections without
understanding them. "

CHAPTER ONE

What Is a Sales Objection?

Y ou can't achieve anything more than minimal sales success if you don't become a master at dealing with objections. Before that can happen, however, you have to understand what they really are and why they come up.

That's important to know, because the salespeople who seem to have the most trouble with objections are also the ones who think they appear randomly out of nowhere. That's just not the case. In the same way that the airline captain I wrote about in the introduction can see storms brewing on the horizon, a great salesperson anticipates that there are going to be a few bumps in the sales process and is ready to deal with them.

In a perfect textbook situation, a customer would express a need, the salesperson would show them how to fulfill it, and then both parties would agree to fill out the paperwork. We all know how rarely that happens in the real world, if it ever happens at all. The obstacles, more often than not, are the objections that our prospects and customers raise.

That brings us to a simple definition. Taking a broad view of things, *an objection is simply anything that stops the sale from moving forward.*

It's really that straightforward. Although there are common sales objections (that we'll examine in this book) and solid reasons that they arise again and again, anything your customer says that could be taken as reluctance to complete an order is an objection. And if you can't remove those objections, the sale isn't going to happen.

Of course, there are some objections you will hear again and again (and probably do already) throughout your sales career. Here are just a few that you are likely to be intimately familiar with already:

- "I'm not interested in that right now."
- "Your price is too high."
- "I already work with one of your competitors."
- "I need faster delivery than you can provide."

There are literally dozens more, but you get the idea. Each of these is a simple objection, and all of them have the effect of stopping a sale dead in its tracks… unless you know how to deal with them.

It's important to note right from the beginning that customers tend to raise objections for one of three reasons. In the first case, it's because they need to convey some important and legitimate information to you (more on this in a second). In the second case, it's because they have real concerns that what you're offering isn't the right solution for them. And finally, some customers will raise objections simply because they want something from you, or to introduce some tension into the sale. In fact, they may even do it just to test you or rattle you.

Understanding these motivations – and being able to focus on why a customer is raising an objection as well as the objection itself – is going to be critical to your ability to work through them. So these are themes we are going to return to again and again in this short book.

Now that we have spelled out exactly what the sales objection is, let's take a quick look at a few of the finer points and distinctions that matter to sales professionals. We can start by looking at a few things that objections *aren't*.

Is It an Objection or a Disqualifying Condition?

Although overcoming objections is a critical sales skill, there are going to be some that you just can't beat. I'll go even further and say there are some you shouldn't *try* to beat.

Every once in a while, I come across a sales professional who prides themselves on never taking "no" for an answer. That's an admirable point of view, and one that can help you develop a good mindset toward closing more business. However, you should recognize that spending time with unqualified prospects is a counterproductive waste of your day.

Some prospects really can't or won't buy from you, and their "objections" might be strong or genuine enough that you should stop trying to win the order. Suppose you sell industrial machinery, and one of your prospects tells you that their company is going out of business, they will soon be laid off, and the company is trying to sell assets just to settle with current creditors. Assuming you believe them, that piece of information should be enough for you to stop pursuing the sale. The customer has given you an objection, and it's airtight.

That's an extreme example, of course, but it illustrates the point that some objections really are disqualifying (at least temporarily). Overcoming objections is about making the most of your time and effort. If it appears that a sale is impossible, then you'll have nothing to gain from pressing the point.

A Sales Objection Isn't Always a Bad Sign

Given that an objection can bring a sale to a grinding halt, they are generally thought of as bad things. It's hard to disagree with that notion, but a good sales professional should know that in some cases an objection can actually be a good thing.

This is especially true early in the sales process. When you're still trying to identify needs or present a solution, having a customer raise his or her concerns can be a positive. For one thing, it tells you that they are paying attention to what you're saying and are at least somewhat engaged in the process. And even better, they are tipping their hands as to the issues that are on their minds.

For example, if a customer tells you, "I don't think my company could afford the payments," what are they really saying? They aren't telling you that they don't have an interest in what you provide, just that they might need different financial terms to make the deal feasible.

Objections are obstacles, but they are also roadmaps telling you how to close a particular piece of business. So the earlier they come up, the better positioned you should be later in the sale.

There Is a Big Difference Between a Question and an Objection

Some salespeople mistakenly think that *any* question raised by a customer is an objection, but that's not just incorrect, but potentially damaging. After all, buyers ask us all kinds of things about the products and services we sell, and many of those questions reveal interest.

For instance, if you're with a customer and they ask you, "Does this come in any other colors?" don't assume that they are telling you that they won't buy because they object to the appearance. Things are just the opposite, and they're mentally taking ownership of the item, wondering if they can meet all of their needs and wants by purchasing.

Again, this is an obvious enough point that most salespeople won't have too much trouble with it. Still, there are some kinds of questions that sound like objections when they are really part of the customer buying process. Learn to spot the difference by paying attention to tone and following the course of the conversation.

A Sales Objection Is Not the End of the Sale

As I've already mentioned a few times, almost *every* sale will meet with some level of resistance between the initial contact and the finished order. That means an important part of your job is recognizing that objections are going to come up and not considering them the end of the sales process.

Although very new or weak salespeople sometimes abandon a sale at the first sign of an objection, this isn't a reasonable course of action. That's particularly true if you've been following a sales process that helps you identify potential buyers who have the possibility of becoming great customers. Assuming you've put a lot of work into finding and contacting the right person, why would you give up just because they aren't sure at first?

When you raise the white flag too quickly, it can be as disappointing to a customer as it would be to your sales manager. Remember that some customers raise objections out of habit, or for reasons that have nothing to do with their willingness to buy. If you hear "no" when they really mean "maybe" or "yes, but…" then you're going to miss out on a lot of great opportunities.

Let's Start Overcoming Objections

We're going to address all of these points in greater depth throughout the remainder of this short book. Even better, I'm going to help you become a master at evaluating the sales situation, understanding the motivation behind a particular objection, and using what you've learned to sidestep them on the way to a finished sale.

As with most things in life, knowing more is the first step toward doing better. Let's take this introductory bit of information about what objections are and see why it's so easy for salespeople to mess up when they hear them in the next chapter.

" *Hearing an objection* *doesn't kill a sale, but the way* **you react to it might.** "

CHAPTER TWO

The 3 Worst Ways to Deal with Objections

Sometimes, the best way to learn how to do something is to see how not to do it first. Or, when it comes to dealing with sales objections, maybe to recognize some existing habits so you'll know what you need to overcome.

Regardless of how you look at it, there are some surprisingly common things that salespeople do in response to objections that can wreck any chance of a sale in the blink of an eye. Hopefully, you aren't using any of these tactics yourself. If you are, though, don't worry – I'm going to show you why these tendencies don't work and how to stop setting yourself up for failure.

To give you an idea of the kinds of habits I'm referring to, and why they are just so damaging to your future and income, let's take a look at the three worst ways salespeople deal with objections.

Bad Idea #1: Further the Objection

This might seem obvious, but if your customer tells you that your product is too expensive (for example), then you can gently acknowledge it, but don't make it a bigger deal than it is.

It's not that unusual to see salespeople furthering objections that buyers raise. Perhaps in an effort to increase rapport, or just avoid conflict, they'll listen to any objection raised by the customer and then parrot the negative idea back to them.

The good news with this bad habit is that it isn't *totally* wrong. It's a good idea to acknowledge sales objections when they arise, but not to make it seem like you agree with them. The difference is as significant as it is subtle. Consider these two conversations, taking place toward the end of a sales presentation.

Here's the first one:

Salesperson #1: "OK, so that's all I have to show you. What do you think?"

Customer: "It costs too much."

Salesperson #1: "I know what you mean. I've told our marketing team that we should consider lowering the sticker price."

Here's a smarter version of that same conversation:

Customer: "I don't know. It really costs a lot."

Salesperson #2: "It *is* a big investment, but what else would you expect from something that took a decade to develop and test? Don't forget that this model is going to save you thousands of dollars every week because it's more efficient than anything else on the market, and it's almost impossible to break. Let me show you something..."

Obviously, there are lots of subtle differences between these two conversations taking place about a fictional business-to-business product. But there are two things that I'm hoping will stand out to you. The first is that salesperson #1 is really shooting himself in the foot by validating the objection. He's unlikely to get the sale, and if he does, it's probably going to be at a significant discount. His more-savvy counterpart still acknowledges the objection, but doesn't reinforce it.

The second point to be made is that the objection is stronger in the first instance, and it is almost invited by the lackluster way in which the salesperson presents his products and then doesn't really ask for the order. I want to reinforce again and again the idea that objections don't come up out of the blue. It's your job to deal with them, but that's easier when you have prepared your customer with the right confidence and mindset.

Bad Idea #2: Bring Up Objections Yourself

Even worse than reinforcing objections is bringing them up yourself. Again, you would assume that this is something most salespeople just wouldn't do, but it happens a lot more often than common sense would dictate.

Staying with our price objection, let's look at how this kind of issue would normally arise.

Salesperson #1, reaching the end of a sales demonstration:

"As you can see, it's a nice-looking piece of machinery. Now, I know it probably costs more than you were planning for your budget, but I'm hoping you'll see that…"

What happened here? In this situation, the customer didn't even object to the price. In fact, he didn't even get a chance to because the salesperson – who was in the midst of tanking his own presentation by ending with what is probably a very weak benefit – just *assumed* that price was going to be an issue and introduced it himself.

Perhaps the client has plenty of money in the budget, or has been looking at more expensive pieces of machinery. Maybe he didn't think it was expensive when they started talking, but begins to wonder if it costs too much now. Either way, the salesperson has put himself in a big hole, again, and is never going to sell what he's offering at full asking price... if he's able to make the sale at all.

You should never presume to know exactly what's going on in a customer's mind, or to guess at things like budgets, priorities, or buying motivations until you have gotten that information directly from them. And more to the point, you should never be the one to raise objections during a sale.

If you don't believe in the products or services you are offering, then quit your job and move to a company that you *do* think provides good value. The best sales professionals like to earn money and awards, but they also feel good about helping their customers and clients to get what they need. You'll have a hard time overcoming objections if you have already internalized them yourself.

Presuming that isn't the case and you do have some pride in what you are helping others to buy, let it show. Instead of worrying (or worse, saying) that your products are too expensive, be happy to talk about all the value your customers get in return. Rather than taking it for granted that others can't afford what you have to offer, make the assumption that they are willing to invest in anything that's worth the money.

Although I'm focusing on the issue of price, because it's both simple and common, these principles hold true for any sales objection. First, never be the one to raise them yourself. And second, don't put thoughts or worries into your customers' minds where they didn't exist before.

It might seem like a big deal to you, for instance, that a buyer has to wait a year to get delivery of something they've paid for, but you don't know what their needs are like, or how it fits into their longer-term vision. By apologizing for something that hasn't garnered a complaint, or raising an objection when one hasn't been expressed, you only turn it into a bigger deal and run the risk of sabotaging your own sale.

Bad Idea #3: Give Up on a Sale Too Quickly

I've already addressed this briefly, and will come back to it again. But it's such an important point that it needs to be stressed in multiple ways, so I can be absolutely sure you get the message: A sale is not dead just because a customer raised an objection.

There are going to be exceptions, of course, but generally speaking objections are simply requests for more information or details that clarify the conditions of a sale. They let you know your customer isn't ready to commit, or that they have two things that need to be addressed before they can sign on the dotted line. That's it.

Just like most flights can't be made in perfect weather, neither can most sales take place without a single objection being raised. You have to be able to accept them, withstand them, and move past them if you're going to succeed in the sales profession. If every objection makes you jittery, or causes you to give away your profit margins on a sale, then you're always going to have a hard time getting by, much less joining the ranks of the leaders in your company or industry.

Objections are just words, and even the toughest ones need to be explored. When a salesperson gives up too quickly, they aren't just losing out on revenue for the company and a commission for themselves… they are also abandoning the time they've spent identifying the prospect and building a relationship. They're saying that they don't believe in themselves, and that they don't deserve the rewards that come with success. That's a lot to sacrifice just because someone else doesn't do exactly what we want them to do, or understand what we wish they would, at the first time of asking.

Although we've already danced around it in these first two chapters, it's time to take a look at the number one sales objection most of us face, and what it really means.

> *Knowing how to deal with the* **#1 sales objection** *you'll hear again and again can* *transform your career.*

CHAPTER THREE

The #1 Sales Objection and What It Means

I t's not exactly an unexpected plot twist for me to reveal, at this point in the book, that "your price is too high" is the top sales objection across every business and industry. Every salesperson has heard it, and most of us will hear it thousands of times before we're done.

But what is surprising is how few salespeople, even seasoned ones, can properly interpret and deal with this complaint from a customer.

You might have noticed that I broke your response to price objections into two parts: *interpreting* the objection and *dealing with it.* It's important to understand what this objection means before you attempt to address it. That's true of all sales objections, but especially ones that come up around the issue of price. Often, they don't have anything to do with costs at all.

Why would customers raise price objections when they can afford what you are selling? Let's get in a little bit closer and examine the issue.

The Real Issue Behind Price Objections

Very often, when a customer tells you that your price is too high, what they really mean is that your product or service is too expensive relative to the value it offers them. In other words, they don't think they are going to get enough in return for what you are asking.

I hate to say it, but that's usually the fault of the salesperson. It's your job to identify good prospects, build enthusiasm, and convey value. Just as importantly, it's your job to explain that value to customers in a way that makes it clear that you have a solution to their need or problem, and not just something that's "nice" in a way that doesn't really pertain to them.

If the customer doesn't think that what you're selling has enough value to justify the price, then it's usually a sign that you've either started the sales process with the wrong person, or haven't done enough to show why your product or service can be the answer they've been looking for.

If someone comes to you with a real need, and you show them the *perfect* solution to their problem or situation – a solution that's better than anything else being offered – their main concern is going to be getting it and putting it to use, not haggling with you over price. So if that's how they are choosing to direct the conversation, then it might be a sign that you need to spend more time building up the perceived worth of whatever it is you want them to buy.

Price Objections Can Be a Smoke Screen

Sometimes, customers will raise objections over price to disguise the fact that they are dealing with other concerns. For example, the issue could be that you are moving through the sales process too quickly and they aren't convinced you have the right solution for them. Or perhaps they have heard some things about your business that didn't leave them impressed. In that case, they may use price objections as a smokescreen for the *real* objection.

Unfortunately, these kinds of price objections can be the toughest ones to deal with because they aren't really about the cost of the product or service at all. But that doesn't mean the sale is lost.

If you suspect that an objection about price is actually standing in for another objection (or that the issue around price might be related to something else), then there are really two courses of action you can take. The first is to make sure you understand what's being expressed. We are going to delve further into this process in a later chapter, but for the moment let's remember that you can always stop what you are doing and re-qualify the potential customer in the middle of the sale.

Obviously, going backward in the sales process isn't as much fun as going forward, but it's better than losing the customer altogether. And really, if you aren't sure that what you're offering is what your customer really wants, then you don't have anyone else to blame when it takes you extra time to close the business. Never forget that the time you spend listening and probing pays off later when you're trying to present a product, ask for the order, and justify your price.

The second way to get around "hidden" objections that are masked by price is to go back to the previous point I made and start building value. Show your customer everything he or she is going to get by purchasing from you, being careful to highlight all the features and benefits that pertain to them individually.

As you begin to create value again, you should either be able to generate interest in the customer's mind or discover what the real issue is through the follow-up questions or statements they give back to you. Either way, you win by making them see just how perfect your products or services are for the needs they are trying to meet.

Another Reason Customers Always Object to Price

Even if you've done everything right in the sales process – having identified a good prospect, built up the value of your product or service, and left them without unaddressed objections or expectations – they may still tell you "your price is too high." That's because they know that issuing this statement can often save them significant amounts of money.

As I've already mentioned, weak salespeople tend to sabotage themselves (and their companies) by giving into objections too quickly. Every customer has worked with this type of salesperson, and will be eager to find out if you are one of them, especially if it's your first time working together. So even if they love your product or service, think the price is fair, and want to get started on an order or account right away, they may tell you that something costs too much to see if it earns them a discount. Years of dealing with salespeople has taught them that this is a distinct possibility.

Your job, of course, is to hold out for the full value of what you sell. If you believe that it's worth what you're asking – and you should – then don't give in. The best way to move these kinds of customers away from price objections is to follow the tried-and-true formula I've given you: acknowledge the objection and then start building value.

Once you go back to talking about benefits and what your product or service can offer, the customer will see that you aren't going to give in easily. Many who want to buy anyway will give up at this point, feeling like they've done their job just by asking. Others may try to negotiate with you for a while, but you'll have set the tone by refusing to give away your margins for no good reason.

How to Prevent Price Objections from Showing Up

It's probably clear to you by now that the best way to stop price objections in their tracks is by re-qualifying a customer and then reminding them of the value you're trying to give them, focusing them on what they will receive instead of what you're asking them to sacrifice. It's only logical that following those steps is the best way to prevent price objections from creeping up in the first place.

Although I've given you some pretty solid common reasons that customers are going to raise the issue of price with you, the reality is that a lot of salespeople invite these kinds of objections by not being thorough enough earlier in the sales process. If you find the right decision-makers often enough, and present your solutions in a customized and impactful way, a fair number of them are going to tell you "I'll take it" before you even get to the price in the first place.

From experience I can tell you that many of the top sales professionals in every industry spend almost no time on price. Although their colleagues tend to think of them as master negotiators, the reality is that they do most of the hard work that it takes to finish a sale long before they ever reach the closing stage. They do such a good job of identifying needs and building value that they don't have to justify budget figures to buyers when it's time to sign on the dotted line.

As with all objections, there *are* going to be times when your price is higher than what a customer has to spend, or when your price doesn't compare favorably to what's being offered by a competitor. Those situations are likely to be rare, however, especially if you're doing a good job of qualifying before you make sales presentations.

You'll never be able to completely eliminate price objections from your day-to-day selling career, but by learning to decipher and overcome them, you remove the biggest obstacle to getting new customers and orders.

"Believe it or not, the right objection can bring you closer *to a finished sale.***"**

CHAPTER FOUR

Advanced Tactics for Strangling Price Objections

Building value into your sales presentation is your first line of defense against price objections, and if you get good enough at it, you'll be able to prevent them from being a serious obstacle most of the time. But because some buyers are likely to do their very best to try to wear you down (if only to get a discount), you need to have other strategies you can turn to.

The closer you get to the end of the sale, the more "dealing with price objections" starts to resemble "negotiating a final price." That's not a bad thing. Although people tend to think of negotiations as an arduous give and take between two parties, they also generally move toward a successful resolution.

If a customer tells you, "Your price is too high," or "I don't want to pay full price," what they are really telling you is that they would like to buy from you, but that they need to see more value or are trying to save some money. Either way, you're closer to a sale then you were before.

Also note that some of the tactics I advise below are just short glimpses into the bigger subject of quantifying things for your customers, which was the subject of my short e-book *Metric Selling*. Because an ROI-based approach can help salespeople see things from a customer's point of view, and to negotiate sales at higher margins, I've included a shortened copy as a bonus chapter at the end of this book.

With that being said, let's look at a few advanced strategies you can follow to counter price objections:

Ask More Questions

If a customer tells you that your price is too high, one of your first reactions might be to ask, "Why?" Assuming they give you an answer that's more substantial than "Because it is," the resulting information is going to be pretty valuable.

For example, suppose they tell you that your price is too high because it's more than they are used to paying. You've now taken something that was vague and made it specific. You can show them that your product costs more, for instance, because it lasts longer or benefits them in a bigger way.

Likewise, a buyer might tell you that what you sell costs too much because they haven't heard of your company in the past and think you are charging premium rates without a reputation. With that insight, you can inform them about the history of your company, the quality of manufacturing components you use, your unmatched warranty, or whatever else there is to justify the increased cost.

Ask questions, and you might be able to get the answers you need to finish the sale at full price.

Comparison Shop

Sometimes, customers think prices are too high simply because they aren't comparing products or services in relation to one another properly. For example, they may not know that many of your competitors, who have a lesser reputation in the industry, are charging even more for something similar to what you offer.

If that's the case, then by all means consider doing a bit of "comparison shopping" to show a buyer that they aren't going to get a better deal elsewhere. You might even want to compare the price of your product or service to others in different industries as a way to make them understand that they are getting good value for what they are spending.

One word of caution: Be careful of introducing competitors' products into the mix before you have properly evaluated the sales situation. The last thing you want to do is send the business elsewhere because you don't stack up as favorably in a key area.

Try Cost Averaging

A lot of the best products and services have a huge sticker price until you put the figures into their proper contexts.

For an easy example, let's go back to the beginning of the book and consider the modern airliner that my airline captain was piloting. Such an aircraft can easily cost tens of millions of dollars, not to mention the ongoing expense of maintenance and upgraded navigational aids.

You could imagine that the executive at the airline who orders the planes will likely say out loud, "Your price is too high," when the manufacturer shows an invoice for a new fleet. And yet, once those costs are broken down into more meaningful figures – like what the aircraft costs per flight, for example, or per passenger – then the purchase suddenly becomes a good one. Things get even better if the newer aircraft can be shown to be faster, safer, or more reliable.

This kind of cost averaging works in almost every industry. Your car is a major expense, but only costs you a few dollars a day if you drive back and forth to work. A new telecommunications system might require an investment of millions, but that could work out to a few pennies per hour for each customer service representative who is employed. Industrial machines have huge sticker prices, but frequently pay for themselves within months.

Find the real average cost of what you sell over a reasonable time frame, and then share those figures with your customer to help them understand the long-term value.

Show a Positive ROI

This ties closely to the last point, only with an emphasis on the money that your customer will either save or earn back when they buy from you. This type of approach is commonly used in business-to-business settings, but individual buyers like to save money, as well, and pointing out efficiency gains can be a good way to earn their business.

The bigger a purchase is, the more likely it is that it will (and needs to) eventually generate a positive return. That return can come in any number of ways, including a high resale price, increased productivity, efficiency gains, less downtime, lowered energy bills, decreased budgets for parts and supplies, fewer labor hours, and so on. Don't just assume that your customer knows how they will achieve a high ROI when buying from you. Spell it out for them, and use good estimates backed up by existing case studies whenever you can.

Point to Durability

Things that last longer are worth more. If a customer can reasonably expect that your product will last longer than what they would buy from someone else, then it's only natural that they should be paying more for it. This isn't a new concept, but it's one that a lot of salespeople misuse and misunderstand.

Unless your company has a very, very good reputation, you're probably going to have to prove the point of durability. And even if everyone is familiar with your brand, you might have to do it anyway.

Let them see for themselves that your products last longer. Show off references, studies, and other forms of proof (especially from third parties, if they are available) that leave no doubt in their minds. Let them know that when they buy from you, they won't have to buy again anytime soon.

Durability is important because it's both a tangible benefit and an intangible one. In a practical sense, having something that's durable means you won't have to spend more money fixing or replacing it for quite a while. In a bigger way, though, it means that you won't have to spend time or stress worried about something that isn't functioning properly, or having to meet with another salesperson anytime soon.

Use the Prestige Factor

If the product or service you sell comes with a high price tag, don't run from it. Instead, do what jewelers and luxury auto salespeople do – embrace the prestige factor of what you have to offer.

Most people don't like spending a lot of money, but they *do* enjoy the satisfaction that comes with owning the finer things in life. They love the way it makes them feel to know they got the best, and enjoy that even more when others can see that they've purchased something that's top of the line.

Although this kind of sales approach is typically reserved for individuals, I should point out that lots of prestige purchases are made at the business-to-business level, as well. In my own industry, I see it when executives are proud to have an event at a prestigious hotel or resort. That reflects on them, and their businesses, in a very positive way.

In the right hands, a high price can sometimes be a feature of a product or service instead of a drawback. Take advantage of the prestige of selling something that's the best, and make buyers feel good about the possibility of owning it.

Make It Emotional

If you have read any of my other books on sales, then you already know that buying is primarily an emotional activity. Although we factor things like pricing, return on investment, and cost averaging into our day-to-day decisions, it's the emotional parts of our minds that tend to drive our behavior most strongly.

Knowing that, you can combat price objections by appealing to the emotional wants and needs that your customers express. Often, "it costs too much" is an emotional response rather than a logical one. Your customer is suddenly experiencing sticker shock and thinking about other things they could spend the money on (either for themselves or their businesses).

By bringing them back to the emotions they expressed early in the selling process, you can once again increase the value of your solution. For example, if your customer has told you, "I *hate* it when my current model breaks. It ruins my schedule for the day and I'm late getting home from work," they have given you some insight into their very real buying motivations. Chances are, your price isn't too high, because what you're offering helps them solve that problem in an immediate and permanent way.

Each of the techniques outlined in this chapter can help you keep a sale moving forward when a customer tells you that your solution costs too much. With a bit of practice, you'll learn how to match the appropriate response to the situation at hand. Then you'll never fear hearing "your price is too high" ever again.

CHAPTER FIVE

7 Other Common Sales Objections You Need to Be Ready For

I f I had to guess, I would estimate that price objections make up more than half of all the objections salespeople hear on average. Simply mastering the right ways to overcome that one issue can help you make more sales and earn a better margin on each one.

Sales objections certainly aren't the only ones you'll get, however, and there are a handful of others you are likely to encounter again and again. In this chapter, we'll look at seven other common objections every sales professional should be ready to deal with.

#1: "I Don't Want to Switch Vendors Right Now."

There is an old saying that people generally won't change their behavior until the pain of what they are currently experiencing outweighs the pain of making some kind of change. A simpler way of saying this is that people don't like doing things differently if they don't have to, even if they feel like the switch would be beneficial.

"Not all sales objections are about price, so you'd better know what customers are **really telling you.***"*

That's one of the reasons why you will often see prospects stuck at a point of inaction. Many people are simply afraid of change, or won't want to upset their normal habits and routines by trying something different.

Usually, this kind of objection is a sign that your customer is too comfortable in the status quo. One way to get them to consider new possibilities is by overwhelming them with the relative value of what you provide. Show that it's worth a lot more, or can benefit them in some tangible way. Another tactic is to point out the risks of not taking action. If passing up your offer could lead to bigger troubles down the road, you might want to point this out in a gentle way.

#2: "The Delivery Time Is Too Long."

This is a tricky one, because an issue about delivery times might not be an objection at all. It could be a customer's way of saying, "If you can get this to me faster, I will buy."

Assuming that isn't possible, your next best strategy is to remind your customer that having the right solution is usually better than taking the one that's directly in front of you, even if it means a little bit of waiting. Do they really want the product or service that's perfect for them, or to buy something they'll end up regretting later?

Another good point here is to remind the customer that, if time is a consideration, then they should place an order immediately so that the waiting period doesn't stretch on for even longer. Buyers who are impatient today are likely to be just as impatient in the future. And their needs might be even more pressing by the time they get around to committing to your solution.

#3: "I Already Buy from My Nephew."

You'll never truly realize how many friends, mentors, and relatives your prospects have until you ask for an order. Then, it seems like everyone has a beloved contact that's in the business.

Believe it or not, this can be one of the best objections you can hear. If a customer is rationalizing the purchases they make from someone else by emphasizing a personal relationship, then it isn't exactly a ringing endorsement for that person's professional skills, or the quality and value of what they sell.

There are a number of ways to overcome this kind of rejection. The simplest is to just remind your customer that they need to do what is right for themselves, not for another friend or relative. Alternatively, you could suggest that your customer keep a smaller portion of the business with their personal contact, as a favor, but get what they really need from you.

Family ties and personal relationships can be strong, but the bigger the purchase is, the more it needs to be based on value. Most businesses and individuals can afford to spend a little bit of money to support a person they care about; very few will want (or have the means to) throw away money or performance for sentimental reasons.

#4: "I Need to Get My Boss to Approve This First."

This can be a tricky one. If the objection is genuine, and your customer really does need third-party approval on the sale, then this is an issue you should have discovered much earlier in the sales process. That way, you could have made a group presentation and involved all the decision-makers at once.

The best thing to do in this situation is to find out who else needs to be on board with the purchase, and then find a way to involve them as soon as possible. Make sure you don't cut your original contact out of the equation, however. For one thing, they should already be in favor of making a purchase with you, and can be helpful in persuading decision-makers higher up the food chain. And for another thing, they might want to be sure they share in the credit that comes from a positive outcome if your solution works out.

Also note that while involving a manager or executive can be time-consuming, this objection can be a real positive because it can lead to further opportunities in the future. The more people you have involved in the sale (and especially at the senior level of a company), the bigger chance there is you can make larger follow-up sales to other companies or departments later.

#5: "Let's Come Back to This in Six Months."

Usually, when a potential customer stalls for time, it's because they are afraid of making a decision. As I've already mentioned, lots of people are uncomfortable with change, and the impulse to keep things the way they are – coupled with the risk of being associated with a purchasing mistake – can lead some buyers to grind the sales process to a halt.

There are a couple of strategies you can follow to spur these kinds of prospects on to take the next step. One is to use the same tactic we encountered earlier and remind your customer about the negative things that might happen if they wait too long to address whatever problem or situation is staring them in the face. Another is to remind them that the sooner they buy from you, the sooner they can start enjoying the benefits of your product or service.

It's important to note that this objection, like objections surrounding price, can sometimes be expressed as a stand-in for other concerns. "I'm not ready to buy right now" could be code for "I'm nervous because you haven't convinced me yet." Obviously, you don't want to twist the customer's arm too much and lose the sale altogether, but a little bit of gentle probing and encouragement can be the perfect answer.

#6: "I'm Not Sure I'm Comfortable Buying from You."

This sales objection can feel like a show-stopper, but it's actually a piece of good news in disguise. When a customer tells you that they aren't sure they want to buy from you, either because they aren't comfortable with you personally or the organization you represent, they are filling you in on an important piece of information: They need to be able to trust you more.

Trust isn't easy to build, and it usually doesn't happen in a matter of seconds, but there are straightforward ways to help customers feel more comfortable. The first is to share testimonials, case studies, and references. Let them know that others are glad to have made the decision to work with you in the past, and you can be counted on to follow through on your promises.

Another technique is to break the sale into a series of smaller arrangements, if possible. Once buyers can get a sense for what it's like to work with you, and see that you can deliver on your promises, they'll start to ease up.

Finally, you can issue written guarantees for things like service and delivery. Although these are the ones that are actually binding, they tend to carry the least value with customers. That's probably because we've all worked with companies that have tried to weasel out of agreements and invoices after the fact. So concentrate on letting your customers know they can trust you first, and then showing it with actual paperwork and documents later.

#7: "I Bought Something Like This Before and It Didn't Work Out."

Although it's expressed in a different way, this objection is really the same one we just covered. It's a worse form, though, because most of us tend to remember bad experiences in an acute and emotionally powerful way.

If you're working with a customer who has been burned by one of your competitors – or even worse, someone from your own company – take things slowly and show them why you are different. Then follow the steps above and go out of your way to show them that they are going to be protected in the event that they aren't happy with their decision to buy later.

Each of the seven sales objections listed in this chapter is fairly common, and they can all be defeated once they are understood. Never forget that objections can actually be a good thing because they clarify the conditions for sale and show that your customer is engaged in the process. When you can see them in that light, you'll have an easier time seeing them subjectively and keeping the sale moving in the right direction.

Although I've given you a few basic ideas for countering each of the most common sales objections, the best salespeople have a strategy that allows them to deal with almost any objection in a way that brings them closer to the completed order and ensures that the objection won't be raised again. We'll look at that plan in the next chapter.

> **Most salespeople don't know it,** but there is a reliable formula **you can use to crush** most sales objections.

CHAPTER SIX

How to Overcome 95% of Sales Objections

We talked about some of the most common sales objections, and good ways to deal with them. As valuable as that advice is, however, it won't help you all the time. That's because some objections won't fall into the categories I've already given you, and others will be presented to you in multiples, or at unusual points in the selling process (for example, a customer raises an objection before you even ask for the order).

For that reason, you don't just need a set of stock responses, but an overall plan for dealing with any objection that is likely to come up when you are working with customers. That's exactly what I'm going to share with you in this chapter.

I gave you a quick preview of this system earlier, but now it's time to explore it in slightly greater length. Here is a proven three-step plan that should help you overcome 95% of all the sales objections you come across:

If the objection seems serious or substantial, though, don't be quick to dismiss it. It simply reinforces the idea, in the customer's mind, that you don't care about their satisfaction and don't have anything helpful to add to the conversation.

So be sure to acknowledge your customer's concern first, if the objection seems like a big stumbling block for them. In fact, you might want to repeat what they said, or ask them if they can clarify.

This can give you a couple of important benefits. Usually, when a customer raises an objection, they expect a salesperson to start talking in an effort to convince the buyer that what they've just said isn't true. Most of us don't like to be told that we're wrong, even when we are, so that just puts customers on the defensive.

By asking your customer a question and listening to the answer, you put yourself back on their side – moving toward an outcome that will help them – and show that you are paying attention. You go a long way toward building trust.

Of course, the more they say, and the more you listen, the better you understand what the objection is really about. This is an issue I'll return to shortly, but it's critical to understand that you can't really solve an objection until you know what it means. Don't assume you know what's on your customer's mind; give them the chance to express their thoughts and feelings directly.

Step 1: Diagnose the Objection

You shouldn't usually ignore an objection raised by a customer. Even if it doesn't seem to be a serious concern, or if the customer is simply testing you (over an issue of price, for example), glossing over something they have said makes you seem uncaring and insincere. Those aren't qualities anyone likes in a salesperson.

Depending on the seriousness of the objection, though, you may be able to sidestep it with some practiced responses. In some sales situations, you might even be able to brush off objections with a quick laugh or a witty quip.

And finally, know that when they are given the chance to speak without being interrupted, some customers will talk themselves out of their own objections. It sounds funny, but I've seen it happen dozens of times. A buyer will raise a concern, think about it out loud for a while, and then conclude that it's probably irrelevant (possibly after asking a short follow-up question or two). If you can let your buyer talk themselves out of a problem, your job as a salesperson will get a lot easier.

Step 2: Build More Value or Resolve the Objection

We have already looked at the concept of building value to overcome issues of price, timing, and competition. It's worth saying once more, though, that almost *any* objection can be melted away if a customer thinks enough of the product or service they are investing in. If you absolutely have to have something, for yourself or your company, it doesn't matter how much it costs or how long you have to wait. Get buyers excited, and the concerns they have will seem less severe.

I should also point out that overcoming an objection doesn't necessarily have to involve multiple points, theories, or explanations. For example, if your customer has seen a model of your product in blue, and would prefer red, give them a red one. If they need service on a specific date and that can be provided, give it to them.

Occasionally, I will see salespeople who are so focused on winning an interaction that they miss out on the opportunity to quickly and inexpensively please a customer. Or they'll push a product or service that isn't the best fit because they want to win a contest or earn a slightly higher commission. These approaches are inefficient because they lengthen the selling process. They also decrease the odds of getting a referral or testimonial from the buyer later. If you can resolve the objection directly without too much effort, go ahead and do so. It will be worth it in the long run.

You'll have to be a little bit careful of taking things head-on, though, if only because of the fact that buyers so often hide their real objections behind other complaints. If you find that you are able to resolve two or three objections directly and your customer still keeps raising other concerns, take that as a strong hint that they might have unspoken reasons that are keeping them from completing the sale.

Step 3: Ask for the Order Again

Once you feel that you have addressed your customer's concern, stop talking and *ask them for the order again*. Many salespeople are afraid to ask for an order once, and will be shy about looking for a completed sale after a customer has raised a concern.

In reality, though, the opposite should be true: If someone has told you what is keeping them from buying, and you can provide a satisfactory answer for their worries, wouldn't the next logical step be for them to complete the purchase? Isn't that exactly what they would want to do?

As I've already covered, you don't want to brush through the concerns that your customers have, or ignore the questions they ask you. But if you're getting verbal or nonverbal cues that they understand how you can resolve the issue, and you've been continuously building value throughout your explanation, they should be prepared to take the next step.

One variation on this approach that can work quite well is to resolve an objection, and then ask your customers if they have any *further* questions or concerns before moving on. On the one hand, this can seem like it's inviting another objection to creep up out of thin air. But, on the other hand, it can show (once again) that you are committed to helping them find the best solution possible.

My advice is to read the situation. Keep in mind that contrary to popular belief, the very best salespeople don't succeed because of what they say, but because of the way they listen and pay attention. If your buyer seems satisfied and ready to move on, ask for the order. If not, give them a chance to let you know what they are thinking about. This is a good idea in any point in the sales process, but it's especially helpful as you get closer to the decision point.

There's no magic in overcoming objections. It's not a matter of being slick or talking your customer in circles. Instead, it involves figuring out what's causing the resistance and clearing up any issues or misconceptions that remain. Any salesperson can learn to do it with just a little bit of focus and practice.

CHAPTER SEVEN

How to Unstick a Sale

If you were to learn, practice, and follow what I've shown you up to this point about recognizing and overcoming objections, you would have the tools you need to get through almost any everyday objection. But what happens when a customer raises an issue you weren't prepared for, or they give you a run-of-the-mill objection and your counter-tactics don't work?

When that moment arrives, you really have two good options. I'm going to discuss the first one in this chapter.

Sometimes, even when you've done a good job identifying and presenting to a prospect, you run into a situation where the sale is essentially "stuck." The buyer has raised an objection and you can't seem to sway them.

It's important that you not become frustrated in this type of instance. Remember that customers don't delay sales to aggravate you – they stop the selling process because they

> *My simple trick for un-sticking a sale* ***can help you double*** *your commissions every month.*

have needs, fears, or worries that haven't been addressed yet. And, as always, the fact that they are willing to keep engaging you despite these details is always a good sign.

Another reason to keep your efforts up is that the biggest sales are the ones that are most likely to come to a standstill at some point or another. They have lots of details, moving parts, and negotiation points. It's only natural that the customer spending $5 million of their company's money, for example, is going to have more objections than someone who is merely spending a few thousand.

Besides, there is a big difference between a sale that's "stuck" and one that's "dead." Let's see how you can get things moving in the right direction again.

Your Secret Sales Weapon: A Clean Sheet of Paper

Those who have attended my seminars, read my books, or gotten training in The MODERN Sales System will already be familiar with this technique. If you haven't, or if it's been a while since you learned about it, a quick refresher is in order.

I like to advise salespeople, when asking customers about their needs and wants, to take out a clean sheet of paper and start making notes as a prospect talks. Doing so focuses the salesperson's attention, shows the customer that the salesperson is *paying* attention, and provides a written reference that can be used during the presentation and closing steps later on.

Thousands of salespeople have used this technique to great effect. It helps them to concentrate, and customers love it when you are focused enough on their needs to take notes by hand.

But while the clean sheet of paper technique is usually thought of as something in the Organize (or Information and Qualifying) step of the sales system, it can be enormously helpful with overcoming objections, too. One of the rules of my sales system is that if you can't go forward, go backward. And an objection is really just a customer's way of saying that you don't have enough information to finish the sale yet. The answer, in both cases, is to step back and pull out a new clean sheet of paper.

To see how this would work in an actual selling situation, suppose a salesperson has just asked for the order, been rebuffed with a sales objection, and used one of the techniques in this book in an attempt to overcome it. But the customer still isn't ready to make the final decision. Instead of becoming frustrated or trying to push ahead without the customer's agreement, a smart salesperson could say something like this:

"Mr. Prospect, I understand that you aren't ready to make a decision yet. It seems like there might be something else that we need to talk about before we can be sure we have the right answer for you. Would you mind if I asked you a few more questions..." (while pulling out a clean sheet of paper).

Very few potential customers, if they have stayed with you this long through the sales process, are going to have problem with providing a little more information.

The Hidden Value of This Approach

Even though this is a simple statement, there are a lot of different things going on. For one thing, the salesperson is slowing down, easing off the pressure, and allowing the prospect to express himself or herself while feeling comfortable. And they are building trust by focusing on the customer's needs, rather than pushing forward to close the sale.

Also, the salesperson is getting a chance to re-evaluate things as they sit. They can ask themselves whether it's possible that they have somehow chosen and presented the wrong solution, or if something has changed in the customer's mind (or the selling situation as a whole) that may mean a new product or service is called for.

Getting more information also increases the odds that the salesperson will discover the *real* reason the buyer doesn't want to move forward if some kind of false objection has been given. There are all kinds of reasons customers might not be ready or able to complete a sale. They don't always fill us in on the relevant information, and in fact will occasionally hide the truth.

With a clean sheet of paper in hand, we have the one secret weapon that can be used to get at the information we really need and bring prospects around to our side. The only thing we have to do is ask questions, make notes on the answers, and resist the impulse to get in our own way.

Take Your Time Moving the Sale Forward Again

In my books, seminars, and webinars, I have tried very hard to show salespeople that it's much, much easier to listen your way into a sale than it is to talk a customer into buying. That's especially true here. The end of the sale should happen naturally, with a customer ready to buy and the salesperson simply tidying up the details and giving them any relevant paperwork to sign. If that's not happening, then something about the situation is rushed, forced, or otherwise not in harmony.

Trying to talk your way through it is only going to make things worse. Buyers are almost always suspicious of salespeople and our intentions. You can overcome that by focusing on your customer and working hard to help them get what they need or achieve what they want. If they don't feel as if they are being listened to, however, they aren't going to share the relevant information you need to close the sale.

When you are stuck on an objection, it's likely because the customer wants to buy but has something in their mind that's holding them back. By slowing down the sale and pulling out a clean sheet of paper, you can take a step back, re-evaluate, and address the concern that's stopping both parties from getting the resolution they need.

More often than not, that's going to be enough to move you toward a successful close, even if it takes a bit of time. But what about the occasions when it isn't? We'll look at that in the next chapter.

" *Some objections can't be overcome, and*
a smart sales professional knows
when to walk away
from a losing situation. "

CHAPTER EIGHT

Know When to Walk Away

The general attitude in sales departments is that more sales are better than fewer, and any customer who can be closed should be. These are both *mostly* right attitudes, but there are some exceptions. That's why the smartest salespeople know when to walk away from certain objections or situations at the negotiating table.

It can be hard to give up on a sale, especially when you've gotten far enough along in the process to ask for an order. But it can still be the right move in certain situations. In this chapter, we're going to talk about that, and how it affects your attempts to move beyond sales objections.

Some Objections Can't Be Overcome

I alluded to this earlier, but it's good to have a little bit of common sense when it comes to dealing with sales objections. Particularly, to remember that some objections just can't be overcome.

If a customer truly has no money, doesn't have the authority to make a buying decision, or is so happy with their current supplier that they wouldn't dream of making a switch, then you aren't going to change that. In fact, if a customer gives you this information truthfully, then they aren't providing you with a sales objection at all – they are disqualifying themselves and you should pay attention.

The problem here, of course, is that some good prospects will give you these objections when in fact they do have a healthy budget, buying power, and some level of desire. Likewise, other prospects will give you secondary objections to hide the fact that they don't meet these criteria, usually because they want to feel important or save face.

So how do you know when an objection just can't be overcome? The first way, obviously, is by asking lots of questions and making the most of your clean sheet of paper. Additionally, you should be doing as much research as you can on your prospects before asking them to finalize the sale if there is any doubt about things like authority or ability to pay. And finally, sometimes you just have to take a prospect's word for it, if they raise the objections early in the sales process, and then revisit them again later.

Learn to recognize when a sale isn't going to happen and deal with it appropriately. At a certain point, attempting to overcome objections just becomes badgering. That's not good for the relationships you should be trying to build with your customers. It shows that you don't really believe what they say, or aren't listening to their legitimate concerns. It effectively kills the chances that you will be able to make a sale to the same customer later, or that they will recommend you to one of their colleagues. Worst of all, it shows that you don't have enough respect for your own time to stop beating a dead horse.

The fact of the matter is that some conditions are not changeable, at least in the short term, which means that some sales objections actually are final. When that happens, your best choice is to move on.

Some Sales Aren't Worth the Trouble

If, during the process of the sale, your customer raises lots and lots of objections, pay attention to their behavior as you address them. If it seems like you're coming up against an endless number of issues, consider that finalizing the sale might not be worth the time or trouble.

There are a lot of reasons why this might be the case. For one thing, some customers (because of their personality or situation) are going to require a lot of information and hand-holding. For some types of complex selling situations, this might be common. But if you feel like you're spending an inordinate amount of time moving through simple explanations, ask yourself whether the hours you are committing to finalizing the sale wouldn't be better spent elsewhere.

Additionally, a very small percentage of customers can be talked into just about anything... but only for a short period of time. So they may raise one objection after another throughout the process of the sale, until they stop being able to come up with reasons why they can't buy. At that point, they may place an order, only to cancel it later or complain that they were strong-armed into making a decision. This is a waste of time, could cost you money, and might hurt your reputation as a sales professional.

Another reason that a lot of objections is a big red flag has to do with the ongoing time of managing the account. Someone who takes hours and hours to make a simple decision is also likely to pester you endlessly with follow-up questions after the sale.

And finally, customers who have lots of objections – or ones who make price objections repeatedly – may not be worth it because of the margins that are left on the sale after you're finished. If they simply won't buy without a discount, then you might be better off finding different customers. Why bother completing the sale if you're going to do all of the work for much smaller commission?

Salespeople should be positive and think that they have the talent, ability, and solutions to service almost every customer. But that doesn't mean that every sale is a good one, or that all customers are worth the trouble.

Selling Is About Effectiveness and Efficiency

Companies spend a lot of time and money teaching their sales teams to be *effective*. That is, they want to know that their producers can get in front of a qualified prospect and present products or services in a way that is highly likely to result in a completed order. It also involves learning to diagnose and overcome common sales objections to increase orders.

What's often lost in this training process, however, is that the best salespeople are also *efficient*. They aren't just able to put their sales skills to great use, but they know when to do so. In other words, they don't waste time on low-value prospects who are unlikely to make a buying decision or become good customers.

You can be the best presenter and closer in the world, and a master at overcoming sales objections, but you're going to have a hard time making a living if you're always trying to squeeze new orders out of people who can't buy, won't buy, or aren't worth the time and trouble.

Imagine for a moment that there are two sales professionals working together at a company. The first one qualifies very carefully, and identifies five good prospects per week. He is decent at overcoming objections and converts three of those five leads into new sales.

The second salesperson is a master at overcoming objections. But she doesn't do enough to qualify her prospects up front. So she meets with ten prospects per week, but only two of them really have a good chance of buying. She closes both of those, but the rest of her time is wasted.

In this hypothetical situation, we have two problems and both of them are quite a shame. In the first instance, we have a salesperson who is letting 40% of his business slip away because he needs to master the art of overcoming objections. And in the second case, we have a different salesperson who is working twice as hard as the first but is making 50% less.

The moral here is that overcoming objections is critically important to your sales career, but so is learning how to find good prospects and when to walk away. Overcoming objections is a skill that will drastically boost your closing ratios, but that doesn't help if you're always chasing people who aren't going to buy from you.

Don't Give Up on a Sale Too Quickly

This chapter is all about knowing when to walk away from a sales objection or disqualifying condition, but I want to caution you about jumping to conclusions too quickly. Any time you are tempted to let a potential sale go, I would advise you to remember two things: first, that some objections aren't as firm as they initially sound, and second, that very few objections are final.

Is this a mixed message? Probably, but it's also truthful. Sometimes, "We can't afford your product" means the company is in dire financial straits and probably won't ever be able to buy from you. Most of the time, though, it really means something between "I haven't budgeted for that purchase right now" and "We can afford it, but I don't want to spend the money."

The best salespeople are a little bit curious, and quite a bit persistent. They know when to walk away, but they also make sure to investigate things a little bit further and find the answers they are looking for. They don't accept a "no" as being final until they have a very good reason to do so.

Don't struggle endlessly to win a sale you're never going to get, but don't give up too easily, either. You'll be amazed at how many deals can be completed if you're just willing to ask a few more questions or try a different approach.

" *Overcoming sales objections* **is much easier when** *you're prepared for them in advance.* "

CHAPTER NINE

Beating Objections Is About Preparation

Even if you have the best knowledge and technique in the world for dealing with sales objections, you still need one more ingredient to develop powerful skills: *confidence*. You need to be able to use what you've learned in a way that sounds natural and reasonable to your customers, and not like you are reaching or pleading to try to finish a sale.

Confidence, of course, comes from a combination of preparation and practice. When you know what to do, and have run through it dozens, hundreds, or even thousands of times before, you can perform without hesitation. That's true for any skill or endeavor, and especially in the world of sales.

You simply cannot overcome objections if you don't seem confident in yourself and what you're saying. So, in this chapter, I'm going to give you some great advice on developing your confidence so you can be prepared to crush any sales objections that might come up.

Start by Learning

By reading through this book, you've taken an important first step toward understanding what sales objections are, why customers voice them, and how you can overcome them. But if you simply read through it once and never revisit the material, then how long is that information going to stay with you? And how useful will it be when you're fumbling around to remember what you read during a sales call?

To really learn how to overcome sales objections, you have to not only expose yourself to the material, but truly internalize it. There are many different ways to do that, and the method that works for you might not be perfect for the next person, and so on. Over the years, however, I've seen salespeople have great success with flashcards, written sheets of notes, and even audio recordings. You should use any of these (or a combination of them) if they can help you master the concepts in this book.

For example, you could take a stack of index cards and write the most common sales objections on one side. Then, on the other side you could place the reasons behind the objection and two or three good responses or follow-up actions.

With that stack of self-made materials in hand, you could master all of the most obvious objections you're likely to hear in a period of just a couple of weeks by studying for a few minutes in the morning. Wouldn't a dramatic improvement in your ability to open new accounts be worth that small sacrifice of time?

You can't master the art of overcoming objections, or develop confidence in your skills, until you've properly learned them. Let this book be your first step, not the last time you ever think about your approach to sales objections.

Make Practice a Priority

Harry Houdini once explained to an interviewer that magic was more about practice than mystery. The sleight of hand that seemed to come so naturally to him was, in reality, the natural outcome of thousands of hours of careful rehearsal. By the time he took the stage with a new routine, it had become second nature to him.

Smart salespeople make an effort to follow Houdini's example. To produce the "magic" of top sales performance, they practice and rehearse different parts of their presentation and routine again and again.

Putting in adequate practice time can help improve any part of your sales game, but it's particularly important when it comes to overcoming objections. To give a reasoned response to customers, you really do have to have a sense of what you'll say ahead of time. Otherwise, you could find yourself fumbling for a response and either losing the opportunity or taking away confidence... either your own or the faith your customer puts in you.

Although the best practice comes from working with live customers, you can get lots of valuable repetition by working with other salespeople in your office, or even friends and family members. Drawing on my earlier advice, why not create a few more index cards with common sales objections on them? That way, you could role-play with others until you are able to respond to sales objections spontaneously.

Practice really does make perfect, and the more you rehearse, the stronger your performances will be.

Tailor Your Approach

One thing you'll definitely want to do is tailor your responses to sales objections so that they match both your style and the situations you're likely to face.

Although the sales objections outlined in the previous chapters tend to be largely universal, there are some concerns that are likely to be specific to your business, area, or industry. If you know that there are some things customers are going to be concerned about, why not tweak your answers and responses until they are perfect?

Perfect in this case doesn't just mean factual, informative, and persuasive, but also in line with your personality and delivery style. What sounds natural coming from me, for example, might sound forced or canned if you tried to imitate it word-for-word. Part of practicing is tailoring your words to a specific style, viewpoint, and situation.

Keep It Fresh

Have you ever seen a really good standup comedian? If so, you know that they can make incredibly witty and insightful observations that seem like they are off the cuff.

As audience members, we subconsciously know that the performers have written these jokes well in advance of the show, and yet they seem to be spontaneous and we react as if they were. In fact, the comedians on stage have probably told the same jokes hundreds or thousands of times already. They know that coming up with the humorous bit is only half the battle; telling it again and again as if it were fresh is just as important.

Comedians do this because they recognize that they are performers, and practicing things like timing and spontaneity is part of giving a good performance. In many ways, salespeople are also performers, regardless of whether they think of themselves that way. Even though a big part of the sales profession is identifying prospects and sharing information, another part of the job is transferring enthusiasm from one individual to another (or to a group). That's only possible if your words and responses seem like they are fresh and interesting to you.

So, as you rehearse your rebuttals to sales objections, get in the habit of saying them as if you were doing so for the first time. Make sure that you sound like you're interested yourself, and it will be easier for your customers to be interested along with you.

If you really want to make the most of this idea, consider using your smartphone to record your practice. After a handful of sessions, you can go back and look at things like body positioning, facial expressions, and tone of voice to see whether you are conveying energy and enthusiasm. If not, keep practicing until it sounds fresh.

Study Your Progress

Another way to develop confidence and improve your sales technique is to keep track of the outcomes after each customer interaction. It only takes a few minutes to jot down some notes following a presentation, and these notes can do wonders for you over the long run.

For instance, suppose you are meeting with a customer who expresses a price objection. Make a few notes about the context in which it happened, how you countered the objection, and what the ultimate outcome of the sales opportunity was. Over time, you'll start to see trends. Maybe you're asking for the order too soon, aren't highlighting value strongly enough in a personalized way, or are having more success with one piece of phrasing than another.

By keeping a running log of your attempts to overcome objections (and monitor your other sales efforts), you make it possible to see what's working for you and which areas of your technique need improvement.

Confidence Is Everything

A great theater director once told his performers that he first wanted them to rehearse until the material became known. Then, he wanted them to run through it further to the point that it became boring. And finally, he wanted them to keep practicing until their work was beautiful.

Most salespeople don't place nearly enough importance on practice, because they don't understand how preparation affects their confidence. To successfully overcome sales objections again and again requires the ability to see them coming, stay calm when they arise, and deal with them in an efficient way. That can only happen when the technique has been rehearsed and implemented many times in the past.

If you are having trouble overcoming sales objections, it's probably because you either haven't been taught what they mean or don't have confidence in your own ability to move past them. Following the advice in this chapter can lead you past both of these costly obstacles.

The best sales objection
is the one
that's never raised.

CHAPTER TEN

Most Sales Objections Are Avoidable

A master salesperson should be able to overcome almost any objection. And yet, they should spend very little of their time doing so.

That's not as paradoxical as it might sound. In the same way that the airline captain I met would have felt comfortable getting us through a rough storm, he had the wisdom and foresight to go around the worst of the trouble. A true sales professional works in the same way, having the ability to use any of the tactics I've outlined in this book so far to get past an objection, and yet having the savvy to avoid most of them in the first place.

Objections are common, but that doesn't mean they are inevitable. In fact, I would say that a lot of them can be avoided outright. Even if you aren't bringing them up yourself, the way that some newer or weaker salespeople do, you can still be inviting them with the way you approach your craft or deal with customers.

In this chapter, I'm going to give you a handful of tips and tools you can use to make every customer interaction smoother and encounter fewer objections along the way. That doesn't mean they'll go away forever, of course, or that you won't have to learn how to overcome them anymore. It just means that you'll spend more of your time moving smoothly toward a finished sale, which should always be your goal anyway.

Better Rapport = Fewer Sales Objections

The better job you do building rapport with your customers, the fewer sales objections you'll hear. That isn't because people automatically buy from you if they like you (although they probably won't buy from you if they don't), but having rapport *does* make a big difference.

That's because rapport, at its most basic level, doesn't have to do with likability, but trust. If buyers don't feel at ease around you, then they aren't going to tell you what's really on their minds. And they certainly aren't going to share details about budget, decision-making power, and so on. When they aren't willing to be forthright with that information, you end up chasing objections you don't understand, or addressing concerns that aren't the real roadblocks.

You don't want those kinds of problems sabotaging you. Luckily, building rapport and establishing credibility aren't difficult. You don't have to have a secret handshake, or ask endless questions about your prospect's family and golf game. Instead, you just need to look like a professional, be able to look others firmly in the eye when you shake their hands, and, most importantly, let them know that you have their interests in mind throughout the sales process.

That, more than anything, comes down to listening and being attentive. Unfortunately, that's something that a lot of salespeople struggle with.

Slow Down and Sell to the Customer in Front of You

It's amazing how often overcoming a sales objection really just boils down to learning to listen, taking notes, and factoring what the customer really needs into the sales equation. But that can also be harder than it seems if you don't have a lot of practice.

As salespeople, we often get used to paying attention to our inner dialogue. That can be a good thing, because it allows us to stay motivated as we prospect, to move the conversation toward benefits and sets of features, and to draw on our own experience when we are closing or negotiating. However, it can also lead us to "tune out" buyers or make assumptions that aren't necessarily true.

Ask yourself: How many times have you heard a prospect start talking about something and immediately jumped ahead to a conclusion? We've all done it, because many buyers tend to have similar needs and problems, and we often do know what they are going to say, more or less, before they say it.

But when we act as if we already have all of the answers, we stop being engaged with customers, and it gives them lots of subtle clues that we don't really care.

The answer – and one of the best ways to prevent objections from arising later in the sales process – is to simply *pay attention and sell to the customer that's right in front of you*. Pull out a clean sheet of paper, imagine that you are hearing everything for the first time, and really key in on what they are saying. Sometimes, the ideas they raise will actually be new. Even when they aren't, the way a prospect says something could turn out to be important later, and the fact that you are practicing your active listening techniques will make a big impression.

Don't jump to conclusions, and resist the urge to mentally flip ahead (or worse, interrupt your prospect while they are talking). Focus on the buyer in front of you, let them tell you what they think is important, and get the information you need to close the business.

Most Serious Objections Are Ignored, Not Hidden

I want to reinforce the point about active listening in a different way. At different points in this short book, I've made reference to the fact that customers will sometimes hide their true objections from us. That's a part of life, but it's also pretty rare. Most people want help solving their problems, and will give a salesperson they trust quite a bit of information if they think it will get them closer to the best solution.

Given that, how is it that so many objections still seem to be "hidden"? The best answer is that they aren't hidden at all, just that salespeople like to ignore them or skip over potential problems.

A classic example is a situation in which a prospect tells a salesperson early on that his or her company makes large buying decisions through a committee. The salesperson hears this, acknowledges it, and then continues to move through a presentation. Usually, the salesperson does this because they are excited to have a real, live, interested prospect right in front of them. But, they're setting themselves up for failure, because that one person probably doesn't have the power to change buying policies just because they are impressed by a demo.

Similar objections about price, timing, and other details are often raised and ignored very early in a sale. Somehow, though, the salesperson seems shocked and surprised when they come up again later.

If your buyer gives you a very serious objection or condition early on, address it right away. It may take a bit of time and effort for you to alter your approach, or even abandon the sale for the time being, but it's worse to pursue an order that you can't possibly close just because it feels more comforting.

Using a Sales System Properly Eliminates Objections

I would bet every dollar I've ever earned that most sales objections are raised because a salesperson either isn't using a good sales system, or is moving through the steps too quickly. Aside from token price objections designed to get easy discounts, most buyer concerns can be avoided by a professional who knows how to move through the beginning, middle, and end of a sale while taking their time.

This is something that I hear from students and clients all the time. After I've taught them to identify good prospects, find out about key wants and needs, make a personalized demonstration based on that information, and then ask for the order, they are shocked to find that the resistance they become so used to seeing will just melt away.

When that happens, it might feel like magic, but it's really just the application of technique combined with the right information. It occurs because you've taken the time to find a good customer, identify their biggest need, and then show them a way to get it. That's the logical flow of things that should occur when you're using a sales system well, and a chain of events that's almost impossible to duplicate if you aren't using the sales system and are leaving things to chance.

Early on in this book, I told you that there isn't any perfect world where every sale moves seamlessly from the first contact to the finished order without any bumps, turbulence, or sales objections. But sales professionals can make their own lives easier, and stop inviting objections, by following simple pieces of commonsense advice like the ones outlined in this chapter.

No matter how proficient you become at overcoming objections, you're always going to close business faster if you rarely have to deal with them in the first place.

CONCLUSION

Like a lot of things in sales, overcoming sales objections is relatively simple, but not necessarily easy. When you see someone who is a master of their craft do it, it looks natural and logical. When you watch a beginner or someone without confidence, it appears to be an impossible task.

The point I'm trying to make here is that it's okay if you aren't great at overcoming objections right now, or if you try to put the concepts in this book to use and struggle in the beginning. As with anything in life, changing your habits is going to feel a bit uncomfortable at first.

But overcoming objections is a skill that can keep you wealthy and successful if you are willing to put in a little bit of time and effort. A salesperson who doesn't know what to say when a customer objects to issues like price or timing is always close to updating his or her resume; one that can confidently move past common objections can find a never-ending source of new business anywhere.

Don't be fooled into thinking that we overcome objections only for our own reasons, though. The essence of a record-breaking sales career is the ability to find people who need your help and then give it to them. Whatever products and services you are offering, there are customers who can use them, and maybe even desperately need them.

For a variety of reasons, they are going to raise sales objections anyway. That could be because of their own fears, because they are afraid to take action, or because you made a mistake earlier in the sales process and find yourself needing to create more value in order to help them solve their own problem. Whatever the reason, being able to successfully deal with objections is a critical part of that process.

Most salespeople aren't great at dealing with objections. Even worse, they might not be aware that it's a skill that they should be developing. As a result, they lose millions and millions of dollars in commissions over the course of their careers. That money goes to other salespeople who have more skill, or evaporates altogether. When that happens, no one wins.

Every great improvement starts with an intention. Nothing I can teach you makes a difference unless you're willing to learn, and then put the lessons you have picked up into practice. I urge you to make overcoming objections a big priority in your own life and career. Remind yourself that you won't be dissuaded by the first sign of resistance, that you won't give in on your prices just because someone asks, and that you will investigate objections to be sure that you understand them and can address them.

If you can make these promises to yourself, and practice until you have the kind of confidence I want you to grow, then nothing can stop you from reaching your goals. Are you ready to become the kind of salesperson who can get past "no" and open up a new world of possibilities?

BONUS CHAPTER

Overcoming Objections with Metric Selling

I t has been discovered by scholars that the ancient Mayans determined that the Earth wobbled, and that Egyptian astronomers calculated the size of our planet within a reasonable margin of error. Going off of little more than a look at the night sky and a few parchments to write on, they set down long equations that transformed our understanding of the universe.

These stories are fairly well known, and they are great examples of human ingenuity. But lost in all of that is something more important – that each of these discoveries led to improvements in day-to-day life. Our Iron Age friends didn't just stare at comets; they used their newfound knowledge to plant more crops. Math heavyweights like Einstein and Newton might have grappled with relativity and gravity on the side, but they also made solid contributions to tangible fields like nuclear power and the banking system. In other words, numbers might seem like fun for geniuses,

"Never forget that someone else would love **to have the chances** you've already gotten.**"**

but in the end, they can have a massive impact on the way the rest of us work, too.

This is just as true in the business world. Most sales-people I know think of math as something that matters to the men and women in the accounting department. While that's partially true, it misses the point. Not only do the figures that end up on a profit and loss sheet have a profound effect on what and how you can sell, they could be one of the keys to increasing your own sales income.

Ask the average business-to-business salesperson what he or she provides to their clients, and you're probably going to walk into a long answer about high-quality products, outstanding service, or some other intangible effect. But what do these things mean, really? What makes them so compelling that a manager or executive should risk a piece of their department or company's valuable budget to get them?

Except in very rare cases, the answer is going to come down to dollars and cents.[1] That is, the decision-maker in question has to be persuaded that by buying from you, they're going to somehow end up with more money in the process. This is true in just about every business sale, but as we'll see in a moment, it especially applies as you reach higher- and higher-level decision-makers – the men and women who can approve a purchase that's ten or twenty times bigger than you might be used to getting.

---

1   Or pesos, euros, yen, pounds, rupees, or some other currency, as the case may be.

In some ways, that's always been the case. There's no profit in throwing money away, and the executives at the top get paid big salaries to make the crucial investment decisions that can make or break the company for years to come. But in this day and age, ROI (return on investment) has become more important than ever. Global competition, budget cutbacks, and a testy economy are forcing even frontline supervisors to think carefully about the purchases they approve. Put another way, there's just no more room for fat in today's businesses. If you're going to sell, you need to understand how your product or service fits in your customer's revenue stream and explain that to them in a way that's persuasive.

If you're new to ROI, or *metric selling* as I call it, then you're in luck – this short chapter is going to give you a quick guide with everything you need to know to master it. On the other hand, if you've been breaking down the numbers to your clients for years, I invite you to read on anyway. Metric selling is a great tool to have at your disposal, and you might just pick up something new you can use to close more business today.

Like any sales technique, metric selling isn't completely new; superstars have been using these methods to close large orders for a long time. But these days, they're more important than ever. Learn how they work, and you might just open the door to a whole new world of bigger, better commissions.

HOW METRIC SELLING WORKS

If you were the kind of student who never knew why "x" ended up equaling the cosine of "z," then take heart; metric selling doesn't involve nearly as much math as it sounds like it would. In fact, the whole thing is pretty simple: You find out what matters to your client, and then show them how your solution helps – in terms of hard currency.

For instance, suppose your company produces construction equipment. The fact that the client can choose yellow or green probably isn't all that important; pointing out that one of your vehicles, on average, lasts three years longer than your competitors', saving your customer $300,000 in the process, probably is. That's not to say that other factors won't still matter, because they will. At the end of the day, though, those numbers are going to say something to that buyer that nothing in your sales literature could.

The important part of that process isn't breaking out the calculator, although we'll talk about the right way to do that; it's in your mindset. Instead of talking about the things that you think are important about what you sell, you're going to find out what the customer thinks is important, and then *sell it to them in terms that catch their attention.*

At this point, you might be thinking to yourself, "I've been doing something similar to this for a long time." And if you're a true sales professional, you're probably right. In my seminars, I like to make sure that the salespeople who learn from me understand the difference between principles and techniques. Principles are the things you have to do if you want to be a successful salesperson, like listen to your customers and find win-win solutions. Techniques are just methods for doing those things better.

Metric selling is a powerful technique. It's not a new sales system, and it won't be the answer to every sales situation you face. As you'll see in the next section, however, it can make a huge difference when you're selling to your most important prospects.

SELLING UP THE LADDER

One of the things that makes metric selling such a great skill to have is that the higher you move up the company ladder, the more you tend to use it. Let me explain: At the lowest levels of selling, you tend to have clients and customers who are concerned with the immediate features of a product or service. They want the product that doesn't break down, for example, or the warranty that covers them against the unforeseen. Those are perfectly reasonable concerns; if you and your team are going to be using something, you want it to work.

But what about that person's supervisor: the executive who oversees the division, or the company's owner who signs the checks? When they're buying not one or two of your product at a time, but twenty or thirty, what are they thinking about? You can be sure that they still want a quality solution, but they're interested in something more concrete – the bottom line. That's where metric selling comes in. The higher you go in any organization, the more *economic buyers* you're going to encounter.

Quality guarantees and shipment dates may be the language of shop floors and corner offices, but when you move up to the boardroom, numbers speak for themselves. The men and women who make the really big purchasing decisions, the ones that can transform your career with their business, want to know what they're getting for their money. And more than that, they want to know how it fits into their future profit growth.

For that reason, it makes sense to get good at talking about the financial returns your solutions offer. A manager might approve your purchase on reputation or proposals, but the folks running the show have the power to make enormous investments if you can give them a tangible reason why.

The rule of thumb is this: The higher up the food chain you're selling, the more numbers are going to be involved. Metric selling is only one technique out of hundreds, but one that can help you think and speak like an informed player instead of a hopeful vendor.

TURNING THE TABLES

Before we get into the nuts and bolts of metric selling, it probably makes sense to point out one more enormous benefit of this approach: It has the power to massively reduce the number of price objections you'll face in the selling process. While this might not sound as wonderful as making monster sales, it can be just as critical in industries where margins run tight.

We all know already how easy it is for the end of the sale to disintegrate into a tug-of-war between the customer and the salesperson over the cost. And students of my books, seminars, and webinars will already know that the best way to prevent this from happening is by building value into your solution before you ever start talking prices. Well, what better way to do that than by showing your prospect *exactly* how far they'll come out ahead by buying from you?

Here's how that works: Instead of waiting for your client to tell you that your price is too high, and then spending the rest of your meeting time trying to justify what you charge, simply turn the tables while you still have the floor. Find out what's most important to your prospect's bottom line (I'll give you some sample questions in just a moment), and then build these numbers in during your presentation.

As an example, suppose you know that the owner of a business is struggling with high electricity costs. Pointing out that your equipment uses 35% less power than the competition's – equaling a saving of $5,000 a year for each of their factory locations – gives your product a lot of bottom-line value. That's going to come in very handy if they try to get you to discount a few hundred dollars off the delivery price. All you have to do is bring back the numbers, because you've already proven that the purchase will pay for itself.

Of course, this is just one hypothetical example. The point to take away is that metric selling is a great way to increase your sales margins. Few buyers are going to ask for discounts when they've already seen how your solution is going to increase their profits. And if they do, you're already going to have the ammunition to fight it by showing them that your price will be outweighed by the money they'll get back.

PREPARING TO USE METRIC SELLING

As powerful as metric selling is, it's not the kind of thing you're just going to throw out off the top of your head. To really make an impact, you're going to have to lay some groundwork before you actually meet with your customer.

The first step is to get a firm grasp of the numbers in your business. Find out what the relative strengths of your products and services are, if you don't already know, and then figure out how those translate into the bottom line. Are clients saving money with decreased downtime? Does your service require fewer hours of training? Is it delivered faster? These specific questions might make sense for your industry, or they might not. I've included several more that might help in the next section, but these should all be used as nothing more than a starting point. You're just trying to figure out exactly how your customers can make more money with what you sell.

In some cases, you might be able to get that kind of information from your company's marketing literature. Other times, you might need to question your sales manager or a few top clients. No matter where you look, though, make sure you find out how your customers are profiting from their company's investment – and that you can back it up with testimonials, case studies, and other compelling evidence.

Armed with that kind of bottom-line insight, you're going to be ready for the second part of the preparation process: asking your customer questions and paying attention to the answers. If you've got a firm grip on what's important to your clients and prospects, it's very likely that their concerns are going to be close to what you expected. Still, no two businesses are exactly the same, and you can't always anticipate what your customer's needs are going to be.

So, as you ask informed questions about your prospect's needs and wants – always the most important part of the sales process – pay close attention to the wording that they use. Anything they say about *profits, costs, revenue growth*, etc., should set off a tiny alarm in your mind and be written down right away, because these statements could be the key to closing the sale. It's easier for a client to believe themselves than it is for them to believe you, so keep your ears open for their bottom-line questions and concerns.

KEY METRIC SELLING QUESTIONS

As I've already mentioned, questions – not calculators – are the real key to making metric selling work. Getting the customer to tell you where it hurts, and then giving them the correct pill to cure what ails them, is still the focus, just like it would be in any other sale. You just have to remember that, when it comes to owners and senior-level executives, that "hurt" is usually felt in a profit and loss statement.

So, in an effort to get you started, I'm providing you with a list of sample questions that can help you uncover your customer's ROI needs, as well as how your solutions might fit into the mix. Remember that these are only examples. If they work for you, that's great; if not, adapt them to fit your own situation:

- How much do you think this is costing your company every month?

- Have you ever calculated your per-unit cost with this machinery?

- How much could you increase production if you didn't have so much downtime?

- What would be the cost if your current system stopped right now?

- How many employees does it take you to manage that situation? How much do you have to pay them?

- Is this issue costing you any sales or customers? What are they worth to your business?

- How many working hours could you save with a more streamlined system? What is your time worth?

- How much could you save in overtime wages if this could be handled more efficiently?

- How much would you save if you didn't have to replace that product every two years?

- Would better credit terms be important for your division's cash flow?

- What would you do if you could save the money you've been spending on this problem?

- How much money do you think you're losing when your equipment isn't working?

- How important is ROI in your decision-making process?

PRESENTING ROI SOLUTIONS

Assuming that you've taken the time to find out what competitive advantages you can offer your customer, as well as what kind of money they could expect to make or save in the process, then going for the close should be pretty simple. All you have to do is refer to what they told you, point out the relevant numbers, and then ask for the order. If you've done things correctly, you shouldn't run into too many objections – especially on price.

With that in mind, there are three main stumbling blocks to using the ROI approach: trying to use it on the wrong person, failing to touch on the relevant issue, and forgetting to leave some supporting data.

Remember that we said metric selling tends to work on economic buyers – the men and women at the top who think constantly about the bottom line. To them, ROI is the key to nearly every investment decision. They want to make more money than they are spending, and completing the sale is as simple as convincing them that they can do that.

For lower-level managers, however, the numbers might not be as important. It isn't that they don't care whether or not the company is successful, because they do, but that the small variations in price often take a back seat to speed, convenience, their relationship to the salesperson, and other concerns. For this reason, it's often easier to sell to executives than it is to frontline supervisors – particularly if you're trying to get them to see the bigger picture.

The next obstacle is talking about numbers that aren't that important to the customer. If your prospect tells you that downtime is a significant problem, don't come back with a proposal that highlights price savings on your warranty package. Metric selling, like any other technique, only works if you use it to pique the customer's interest.

And finally, take care to leave your ROI proposal – as well as any supporting materials – behind once you've finished. More and more organizations are making their major purchases by committee these days, and it's possible that your prospect will need someone else's approval to complete the order. Make it easy for anyone who steps in to see how the customer is going to make money from working with you.

MAKING METRIC SELLING WORK

If you paid close attention, you might've noticed that there's one special ingredient to the metric selling technique that's incredibly important, but hardly mentioned: *listening.*

Used correctly, this method can be used to open lots of new doors and close dozens of new sales. But for any of that to happen, you're going to need to have the discipline to let your customers tell you what they need. Like I said before, using ROI isn't an entirely different form of selling – it's just a different way to reach higher-level prospects.

If you've read one of my books or attended one of my seminars or webinars, the chances are good that you've already heard me talk about the power of a clean sheet of paper. Simply put, there's no substitute for making notes of what your customers tell you about their problems, the solutions they're looking for, or what they've tried in the past. The difference here is that you are making a special note of any numbers (or bottom-line financial issues) that they mention.

That's because you're going to take some of that data and turn it into a metric selling point. I promised you earlier that there wouldn't be any heavy math, and that's true. In most cases, getting to the ROI is as simple as dividing costs over time, figuring savings in wages paid, or calculating how much more money your client can make by producing more.

In fact, the simpler your math is, the better. Using complicated equations and formulas to convince your client to buy is likely to leave them with the impression that you're trying to hide something. Explaining savings or profits on the back of a napkin or through a simple chart, on the other hand, is a lot more powerful.

And with that, I'll leave you with the biggest secret of metric selling: It isn't that hard. You don't have to be Einstein, an accountant, or even an engineer; you just have to look for the numbers that your customer cares about, and then show them how to improve their business.

I hope that the time you've spent learning about metric selling has been valuable to you. Like all techniques, it may take a bit of practice before you feel comfortable using it. But once you do, the numbers will speak for themselves.

AN EXAMPLE OF METRIC SELLING IN ACTION

By now, you've probably got a good handle on how metric selling and ROI can work for you in a high-level sales situation. But to help you put it to use in your own sales career, I've decided to offer an example from my own business.

A few months ago, a client came to me with a problem. I'm not going to go into specifics, but the biggest issue was that he employed twenty bright, energetic sales producers who weren't developing as quickly as he had hoped. In other words, he was sure he had a good group of personnel, but couldn't understand why he wasn't seeing better results.

As a long-time sales trainer and consultant, this is a situation that I've run into hundreds of times before. After spending a little bit of time with his sales team, it was easy to see which areas would need improvement. But what's more, I knew that my client wasn't really interested in books, seminars, or meetings – he wanted a way to get more out of his staff and improve its financial picture.

To that end, I recommended a consulting package, but not one that focused on the number of presentations I would give, or materials I would provide. Instead, I showed him case studies from past clients, highlighting the specific improvements and ROI that they had enjoyed from my work.

Consider this: The company in question employed twenty sales reps, as I mentioned before, generating an average of $300,000 each per year in new revenue. I was able to show my client that, in the past, similar companies that I had worked with had improved their sales around 7% in the first year following my training. In this case, that would translate into an extra $21,000 per salesperson coming through the door – or $420,000 in new business every twelve months. Viewed in that light, didn't my $30,000 consulting fee seem pretty reasonable? He agreed it was a drop in the bucket compared to the benefits of a transformed sales effort.

Was there anything complicated in that scenario? Absolutely not. And the same thing could work for a number of other metrics like cash flow, interest savings, replacement cost, and so on. This just happened to be the relevant number for me. Find the numbers that work for you in your business. And when you do, use them to take your selling career to a new level.

Carl Henry is a sales educator, keynote speaker and corporate consultant. During the course of his own successful career, he developed The MODERN Sales System, which he has been sharing with companies and associations around the world for many years.

A Certified Speaking Professional and a member of the National Speakers Association, Carl teaches essential sales skills with humor, insight and personal experience. Hundreds of companies throughout a diverse range of industries have used his highly-acclaimed seminars to educate and inspire their sales teams.

Carl's other books include The MODERN Sales System, The PEOPLE Approach to Customer Service and 15 Hot Tips that Will Supercharge Your Sales Career.

He currently lives in Charlotte, North Carolina.

To order additional copies of this book, or find out about Carl's seminars contact him at:

Henry Associates
704-847-7390
9430 Valley Road Charlotte, NC 28270
chenry@carlhenry.com
www.carlhenry.com

To order additional copies of this book contact:

Henry Associates
704-847-7390
9430 Valley Road Charlotte, NC 28270
chenry@carlhenry.com
www.carlhenry.com

33820819R00067

Printed in Great Britain
by Amazon